DK ESSENTIAL MANAGERS

P9-BJD-346

Negotiating

MICHAEL BENOLIEL AND WEI HUA

London, New York, Melbourne,
Munich, and Delhi

Editor Daniel Mills
US Editor Margaret Parrish
Senior Art Editor Helen Spencer
Production Editor Ben Marcus
Production Controller Hema Gohil
Executive Managing Editor Adèle Hayward
Managing Art Editor Kat Mead
Art Director Peter Luff
Publisher Stephanie Jackson

Produced for Dorling Kindersley Limited by

cobaltid

The Stables, Wood Farm, Deopham Road,
Attleborough, Norfolk NR17 1AJ
www.cobaltid.co.uk

Editors Kati Dye, Maddy King,
Marek Walisiewicz
Designers Paul Reid, Lloyd Tilbury

First American Edition, 2009

Published in the United States by DK Publishing
375 Hudson Street, New York, New York 10014

09 10 11 12   10 9 8 7 6 5 4 3 2 1

ND135—July 2009

Published in Great Britain by
Dorling Kindersley Limited.

A catalog record for this book is available from
the Library of Congress.

ISBN 978-0-7566-5043-8

DK books are available at special discounts
when purchased in bulk for sales promotions,
premiums, fund-raising, or educational use.
For details, contact: DK Publishing Special Markets,
375 Hudson Street, New York, New York 10014 or
SpecialSales@dk.com.

Color reproduction
by Colorscan, Singapore
Printed in China by WKT

Discover more at **www.dk.com**

Contents

CHAPTER 3

Conducting negotiations

CHAPTER 4

Developing your technique

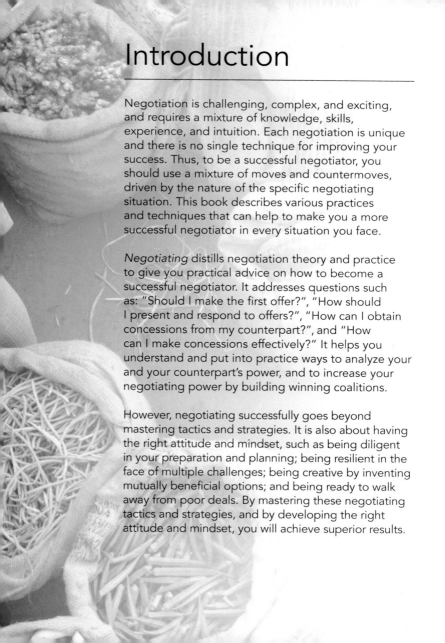

Introduction

Negotiation is challenging, complex, and exciting, and requires a mixture of knowledge, skills, experience, and intuition. Each negotiation is unique and there is no single technique for improving your success. Thus, to be a successful negotiator, you should use a mixture of moves and countermoves, driven by the nature of the specific negotiating situation. This book describes various practices and techniques that can help to make you a more successful negotiator in every situation you face.

Negotiating distills negotiation theory and practice to give you practical advice on how to become a successful negotiator. It addresses questions such as: "Should I make the first offer?", "How should I present and respond to offers?", "How can I obtain concessions from my counterpart?", and "How can I make concessions effectively?" It helps you understand and put into practice ways to analyze your and your counterpart's power, and to increase your negotiating power by building winning coalitions.

However, negotiating successfully goes beyond mastering tactics and strategies. It is also about having the right attitude and mindset, such as being diligent in your preparation and planning; being resilient in the face of multiple challenges; being creative by inventing mutually beneficial options; and being ready to walk away from poor deals. By mastering these negotiating tactics and strategies, and by developing the right attitude and mindset, you will achieve superior results.

Chapter 1

Preparing to negotiate

Negotiation is a skill that you can learn and develop through practice and experience. By framing the process correctly and by searching in advance for creative options, you will be able to find solutions that satisfy the interests of all parties.

Becoming a negotiator

Many people shy away from negotiation because they think it implies conflict. In fact, negotiation is what you make it. When undertaken with confidence and understanding, negotiation is a creative interpersonal process in which two parties collaborate to achieve superior results.

Seeing the benefits

When you become skilled in negotiation, you can create real value for your organization. Negotiation allows you, for example, to secure cost-effective and reliable flows of supplies, enhance the financial value of mergers and acquisitions, settle potentially damaging disputes with union leaders or government officials, or resolve internal conflict constructively. Negotiation is increasingly recognized as a core competency. Many companies develop their own methodologies and offer training and mentoring programs for negotiators.

Understanding the basics

Good negotiators are made rather than born. Although some may be naturally gifted and intuitive (possessing, for example, the ability to empathize with others), most have developed their principles and tactics over time and recognize that negotiating is a largely rational process.

To be a successful negotiator, you have to feel psychologically comfortable in the negotiation situation. This means being able to tolerate uncertainty, deal with unexpected behavior, take measured risks, and make decisions based on incomplete information. You need to think about solving problems and creating opportunities rather than winning or losing: if you are confrontational, you are likely to have a fight on your hands. And if you "win" there will necessarily be a loser, with whom you may have to work in the months to come.

TIP

LEARN YOUR ART

Developing the skills needed to be a successful negotiator can take time, so be patient. Try to learn from every negotiation you undertake, both for your organization, and in your life outside work.

BUILDING A FOUNDATION

FAST TRACK	OFF TRACK
Keeping an open mind to learning new techniques	Believing that negotiating is an innate ability
Treating negotiation skills as a mixture of rationality and intuition	Negotiating from a fixed viewpoint
Developing trust slowly	Appearing too eager
Expressing empathy while negotiating assertively	Behaving assertively without expressing empathy
Having a strategy and sticking to it	Chasing haphazard opportunities

Understanding negotiation dilemmas

The negotiating task is very complex because it embodies a number of fundamental dilemmas. To be successful in your negotiations, you need to understand the difference between the true dilemmas that you need to address, and the many myths that surround negotiating.

Identifying true dilemmas

Over time, a number of myths have evolved about the nature of negotiations. Many negotiators continue to hold to them, failing to recognize the difference between these myths and the real dilemmas they face. For example, it is a popular misconception that a negotiator must either be consistently "tough" or consistently "soft" if they are to be successful. In reality, effective negotiators do not need to choose between these approaches, but are flexible and use a repertoire of styles.

THE STRATEGY OR OPPORTUNITY DILEMMA
Unexpected opportunities sometimes arise in negotiation. It can be tempting to divert from your well-planned strategy, but be aware that this may distract you from achieving your objectives.

Many also believe that negotiation is largely an intuitive act, rather than a rational process. It is true that an effective negotiator will use their intuition to a certain extent (to know the right moment to make a concession or present an offer, for example). However, most of the negotiating task requires systematic processes such as masterful due diligence, identifying interests, and setting clear objectives.

Skilled negotiators are able to recognize the myths and focus their energy on the true negotiation dilemmas, balancing their approach and making the difficult decisions needed to achieve the most successful outcomes in their negotiations.

THE HONESTY DILEMMA

How much should you tell the other party? If you tell them everything, they may exploit the information and take advantage of you, so you need to strike a balance between honesty and transparency.

THE TRUST DILEMMA

Trust is needed for a negotiation to move forward, but if you trust the other party completely, you put yourself at risk of being taken advantage of. Invest in building trust, albeit with measured caution.

The five negotiation dilemmas

THE EMPATHY DILEMMA

If you develop empathy with the other party, it may stop you from acting assertively and negotiating for your interests. Try to do both well—maintain good relationships, but protect your interests too.

THE COMPETE OR COOPERATE DILEMMA

You must compete for the benefits on the table, but also cooperate to create them with the other party. You therefore need to be skilled at both, to be able to create and then claim value.

Being prepared

Your success in a negotiation depends largely on the quality of your preparation. Start by thinking through your position and your objectives. Having clear goals will protect you from making too many concessions and motivate you to perform better. Objectives should be specific, quantifiable, and measurable. Only then can they be used as benchmarks to measure your progress during the negotiation process.

TIP

VALUE THE ISSUES
Draw up a list of potential negotiating points, starting with the most critical. Give each issue a value, and estimate the value that your counterpart is likely to place on it.

Setting the limits

You should always go to the negotiating table with clear answers to the following questions: why do you want to negotiate the deal? How will this deal create value for you? What are your "deal breakers"? What must you have from the deal, what would you like, and what are you willing to give away? There may be alternative outcomes that you can accept—what are they?

Knowing your objectives

Set your objectives high but not outrageously so. It is tempting to censor your aspirations, setting them too low to protect yourself from the prospect of failure, but in doing so, you will almost certainly achieve less than was possible. If you fail to set clear objectives, there is also a danger that you could get trapped in an "escalation of commitment"—an irrational urge to "win" the negotiation at any cost.

Escalation of commitment is a real hazard in negotiation, and happens when you refuse to give up your pursuit of a negative course of action when the wiser choice would be to cut your losses and move on. Always set a limit for how far you are prepared to go and prepare an exit strategy (a means of walking away from the deal).

IN FOCUS... AVOIDING ESCALATION OF COMMITMENT

It can be easy to fall into the trap of competing with the other party at all costs, to ensure that you get that "win." For example, in the late 1980s, Robert Campeau, a Canadian businessman, made a hostile bid to acquire Federated Department Stores (FDS). Macy's, a competitor of FDS, was also interested and a bidding war began between Campeau and Macy's.

Determined to win, Campeau kept increasing his already high bids to a point where he offered to pay an additional $500 million. Campeau won the competition, but two years later he declared bankruptcy. This is a classic case of escalation of commitment, and a lesson for all negotiators in keeping a sense of perspective in their negotiations.

Looking across the table

TIP

DO THE RESEARCH

Information is power. Find out as much as you can about your counterpart before you sit down to negotiate.

A negotiator was once asked if he could formulate a proposal that took into consideration both his and his counterpart's interests. He was puzzled. "Why should I care about the other party's interests?", he asked, "His interests are his problem." Such an attitude of blinkered self-interest characterizes the unprepared negotiator. In order to succeed, you not only need to understand yourself and your interests, but also the other negotiating party, and the situation as a whole. Ask yourself the following questions when preparing for a negotiation:

• Who will come to the table? Research their personality, and their history of negotiation. Have they been previously successful or unsuccessful and what approaches did they use?
• What can you find out about their negotiating style, life history, hobbies, and interests?
• If you have more than one counterpart, do they share the same backgrounds and functional area, and are they likely to be united in their desired outcome?
• Are they authorized to make binding decisions? If not, who are the "players" behind the scenes who will make the final decision?

Understanding your counterpart

It is important to understand the issues and interests of the other party before you start the negotiations. Negotiators come to the table because they each need something from one another, so you must identify your counterpart's key issues and interests. How important is each one? Which are the deal breakers and which may they be willing to concede?

Try to assess whether it is you or your counterpart who holds the power. What are your counterpart's strengths and weaknesses? What is their level of information and expertise? How badly do they want to make a deal with you? Do they have other attractive options? Can they walk away from the table and exercise a BATNA*? Are they pressed for time? If you know that the other side has a tight deadline that you are able to meet, you may be able to negotiate a better price. Similarly, if you know that your counterpart has recently expanded production capacity, you may be able to gain better terms for larger volumes of orders.

*BATNA — *acronym of Best Alternative To a Negotiated Agreement. This term is used by negotiators to describe the course of action that you (or your counterpart) will take if negotiations break down.*

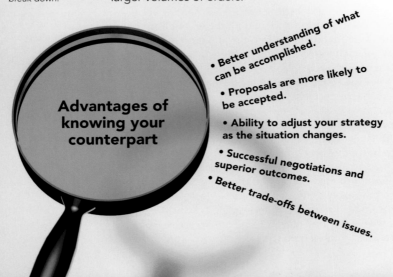

Advantages of knowing your counterpart

- Better understanding of what can be accomplished.
- Proposals are more likely to be accepted.
- Ability to adjust your strategy as the situation changes.
- Successful negotiations and superior outcomes.
- Better trade-offs between issues.

Thinking strategically

Much of what occurs in the negotiating room is, in fact, determined by what happens outside the negotiating room. This requires you to think strategically about your situation in relation to the situation of your negotiating counterpart. For example, in some negotiations, you and the other party may be representing others. Make sure you are very clear about the identity of your constituency, and that of your counterpart. What are their expectations and can you influence them?

If there are several negotiating parties, analyze all of them and begin to think in terms of coalitions. With whom and how can you build a winning coalition and how can you block a threatening coalition?

TIP

CONSIDER THE TIMESCALE
Shape your negotiating strategy with respect to the timescale. You can be more blunt in a short, one-off negotiation than in a long negotiation that is part of an ongoing relationship.

Tailoring your strategy

Make sure that your negotiating strategy and behavior reflects the other party's situation and approach. For example, in many negotiations, the other party is free to leave or join the negotiating table as they wish. In some cases, however, the parties are bonded together over the long term and cannot simply walk away, and your strategy should reflect this.

Some negotiators prefer to negotiate away from the public eye, while others insist on keeping all stakeholders and the public informed. Consider which mode is more advantageous to you, taking into account the sensitivity of the issues, the history between the parties, and the legal and governance systems of each party.

Some negotiation counterparts observe formal protocols in negotiations, while others are freer in what can and cannot be said. Take particular care to do your research when negotiating internationally to learn the formalities expected of you.

Designing the structure

Before producing a blueprint for a building, an architect first studies the functionality of the structure—the purpose it will serve. When you are planning a negotiation, you need to think like an architect and devise a structure and a process that will best fit the purpose of the negotiation.

TIP

CREATING THE RIGHT TEAM

In team negotiations, carefully consider the size and composition of your team so that you include all necessary skills and represent all key constituents.

Structuring your approach

Every successful negotiation starts with a clear structure: defined roles, agreed rules, a set agenda, and a schedule for action. A framework for the negotiation will most likely be suggested by each of the participants. It is then subject to negotiation and joint re-creation so that all parties are satisfied that it reflects their concerns. Consult with your opposite number before you negotiate to agree all procedures that you will use. If you cannot agree on the procedures, it may be better to postpone or abandon the negotiations altogether.

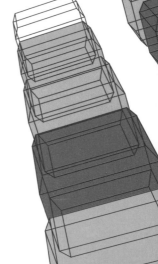

Making a framework

Your agreed framework needs to be sufficiently flexible to accommodate changes in circumstance, but should at very least cover the following:

• **Basic ground rules** These need to be agreed with your counterpart. For example, is it acceptable to change negotiators in midstream? Are observers allowed? Is the meeting open or closed? How should people be addressed and how should priority of speech be given? What will be the course of action if you cannot reach agreement?

All parties should agree to listen respectfully to one another, attempt to understand the positions of others, and refrain from legal proceedings for the duration of the negotiation.

• **A clear agenda** This should include all the substantive issues and interests that you and your opposite number wish to negotiate. Clarify the level of importance of each issue and decide the order in which issues should be discussed. Some negotiators prefer to start with easy issues, others tackle everything together.

• **An agreed venue** Chinese philosopher Sun Tzu's *Art of War* states that one should "lure the tiger from the mountain"—that is make your counterpart leave their comfortable environment. Ask yourself how the choice of venue will affect you and your team. At the very least, ensure that you will have access to the necessary support (computers, secure phone lines, and advisors).

Managing processes

Once you have an agreed framework in place, you also need to structure the processes that will steer the negotiation through its various phases. There are three distinct processes—the negotiation process, the temporal process, and the psychosocial process—that come together in any negotiation. Each requires a different set of skills.

The negotiation process involves managing information and communications during the discussions, planning and re-planning, coordinating efforts between negotiators, making moves and countermoves (all in real time), and making important decisions under conditions of uncertainty and time pressure.

Keeping time

The temporal process involves managing time and the way in which the negotiation moves from one stage to the next by appropriately pacing the speed of each stage and synchronizing the actions of the negotiators. Many negotiations (and sales presentations) stall because the negotiators labor points for too long and are unable or unwilling to move the process toward its closure phase.

Thinking straight

The psychosocial process requires a sound knowledge of human behavior and an understanding that people will take on "roles" during negotiations. You need to be able to overcome barriers to rational negotiation and avoid psychological traps, such as the illusion of optimism, a sense of superiority, and overconfidence. Other hazards include a reluctance to reverse a decision that produces poor results or intense conflict, and competition between negotiators in the same team.

Playing by the rules

The purpose of processes and structures is not to constrain the progress of the negotiation, but to give you tools to resolve challenges or impasses. Having clear rules will allow you to:
• Move from multiparty negotiations to one-on-one negotiations.
• Change the level of negotiation, upward or downward.
• Replace negotiators who are self-serving or too rigid.
• Expedite the process by issuing a deadline.
• Change the venue or schedule.
• Conduct some of the negotiations behind the scenes by introducing a back channel.

Avoiding common mistakes

Never underestimate the risks associated with poor preparation: when you fail to plan, you plan to fail. The most common errors in forward planning include:

RELYING ON SECONDARY INFORMATION

Always seek out reliable sources of primary information. By all means read industry report analyses, reports of management projections, and corporate annual reports, but consider that these reports may sometimes be inaccurate or biased.

AVAILABILITY BIAS

It is easy to find information that is widely available. Make an effort to uncover information that is not so easy to obtain.

CONFIRMATORY BIAS

Do not filter out important information because it does not fit with your existing points of view and beliefs.

INFORMATION ASYMMETRY

Do you really know as much as you think? To be safe, you should assume by default that you know less than the other party.

OVERCONFIDENCE

If you underestimate your counterpart you will neglect to plan well. If you already think you know how a negotiation will end, you may exclude new sources of information and creative solutions.

UNDERESTIMATING RESOURCES

In any negotiation you must be able to present supporting facts, anticipate how the other side will respond to your arguments, and prepare counterarguments. Do not underestimate how long it can take to assemble such information, especially if you require input from experts and colleagues.

Chapter 2

Setting your style

There are many approaches to negotiation. Some negotiators advocate a hard-line, uncompromising style. Skilled negotiators know that you are more likely to achieve a satisfactory outcome by taking the interests of the other party into account and trying to create win–win deals, develop mutual trust, and build relationships for the future.

Defining negotiation styles

Negotiators come to the negotiation table because they have needs that they believe may be fulfilled through negotiations. In order to fulfill these needs, negotiators use different styles and engage in a variety of behaviors that they trust will help them get what they want.

Value-claiming behavior — competitive actions undertaken by a negotiator in an attempt to ensure a win–lose outcome in their favor. Such actions include making excessive demands or threats, concealing interests, and withholding information.

Spotting different approaches

There are three styles of negotiation: distributive, integrative, and mixed motive. Negotiators that use the distributive style view negotiations as a competitive sport, a zero-sum game with a winner and a loser. Such negotiators compete fiercely for the distribution of the outcomes (the size of the pie) and engage in value-claiming behavior*. They dismiss the value of building relationships and trust as naive, tend to use threats to obtain concessions, and exaggerate the value of the small concessions that they make. They also conceal their needs, do not share information, do not look for possible creative ideas, and even use deceptive tactics. In contrast to value-claiming negotiators, integrative negotiators believe that the size of the pie is not fixed and can be expanded, and that the negotiation process is able to produce a win–win solution. The integrative style of negotiation is designed to integrate the needs of all the negotiators. Negotiators engage in value creation behaviors. They invest in building relationships and nurturing trust, share information openly, and are cooperative, flexible, and creative.

TIP

TAILOR YOUR APPROACH
Utilize all of the negotiation styles—distributive, integrative, and mixed—where appropriate, depending on with whom you are negotiating and what their negotiating style is.

Using mixed-motive tactics

The true nature of effective negotiations is often mixed, requiring both cooperative and competitive tactics. The rationale for this is that, through cooperation, negotiators create value; they put money on the table. Following this, once value has been created and the money is on the table, the parties have to split it among themselves. In order to secure the most profitable split, a negotiator has to switch from the cooperative mode to the competitive mode.

 IN FOCUS... RESPONSES TO DISTRIBUTIVE TACTICS

If the other party is using a distributive win–lose approach, a negotiator who favors the win–win style must protect their own interests. Some respond with the same hard tactics, meeting toughness with toughness. However, since the win–lose negotiation style is most likely to produce sub-optimal outcomes, it is advisable to first try to influence the other party to move toward a more integrative style.

Value claimants often think the other party is oblivious to their tactics, and so some negotiators inform the other party tactfully but firmly that they know what they are doing and that it doesn't contribute to productive negotiations. If all approaches to dealing with value-claiming tactics fail, however, and if they do not require the deal, many negotiators will simply leave the table.

Defining interest-based negotiation

Negotiators often make the mistake of turning the negotiation process into a contest of positions. Some are hard bargainers, thinking of the other party as an adversary; others take a soft approach, considering the other person to be a friend and making concessions easily. Instead of utilizing hard or soft bargaining tools, effective negotiators tend to focus on the interests of both parties.

Focusing on interests

In interest-based negotiation, the negotiators come to the table with a clear understanding of what they want and why they want it, but also with an understanding that the other party has its own set of needs to fulfill. Knowing that both parties' needs can be satisfied in multiple ways allows for the negotiation process to be more about constructive problem solving—that is, collaborating to find out what they can do together in order to achieve their respective interests.

Focusing on interests involves concentrating on the "why" instead of the "what." People always have a reason for wanting something. For example, imagine that you and your friend are arguing over who should have the last orange in the fruit bowl. Your friend may want the orange because she wants to make juice, while you may want it because you need the peel to make cake. If, rather than arguing, you talk about why you need the orange and uncover the underlying interests behind your respective positions, you will discover that one orange can satisfy both of you.

> **AIM FOR JOINT GAINS**
> Instead of limiting the thinking to only one or two options, work jointly with the other party to creatively explore many potential solutions.

> **SEE BOTH SIDES**
> Assess the situation from the other party's perspective. This improves communication and helps the other party understand how they stand to benefit from the deal.

Conducting interest-based negotiations

SEPARATE THE ISSUES
Keep people issues, such as emotions, separate from substantive issues (such as price or delivery dates).

FOCUS ON INTERESTS
Make sure that you have a clear understanding both of your own interests and those of the other party.

EXCHANGE INFORMATION
Before making any decisions, exchange information with the other party in order to jointly explore possible solutions.

KNOW YOUR BATNA
Make sure that you have a clear understanding of your BATNA (Best Alternative To a Negotiated Agreement)—the best option available to you if the negotiation process falls apart.

USE STANDARDS
Base your negotiation on precedents, laws, and principles, rather than arbitrary judgements. This makes the agreement fair and makes it easier to explain the rationale to others.

Negotiating from the whole brain

We all think differently, and naturally bring our own "style" to the negotiating table. Understanding the strengths and weaknesses of your thinking style, and tailoring your approach to take into account the style of your counterpart, can greatly improve your success in negotiation.

Understanding your own style

Ned Herrmann, author of *The Creative Brain*, proposed that there are four thinking styles: the rational self, the safekeeping self, the feeling self, and the experimental self, which relate to dominance in different quadrants of the brain. Negotiating is a whole-brain task, requiring the ability to be diligent and rational (quadrant A activities), to plan and organize well (quadrant B activities), to interact well with others (a quadrant C trait), and to be bold and take risks (a quadrant D characteristic). However, only four percent of the population is dominant in all four quadrants. Most negotiators, therefore, have strengths and

CHECKLIST **UTILIZING THINKING STYLE DIFFERENCES IN NEGOTIATION**

	YES	NO
• Have you determined what your own thinking style is?	☐	☐
• Have you identified your weaknesses in negotiation and are you working to improve in those areas?	☐	☐
• If putting together a team of negotiators, have you taken each person's thinking style into account? Do they complement one another?	☐	☐
• Are you able to quickly assess the thinking style of others?	☐	☐
• Do you take your counterpart's thinking style into account when negotiating with them?	☐	☐

weaknesses in performing the negotiating task, and should work to improve in their weakest areas. A negotiator who has limited abilities in the feeling self (quadrant C), for example, can improve by developing his or her emotional intelligence. A negotiator who has limited abilities in the experimental self (quadrant D) can improve by developing his or her creative abilities by taking creativity workshops.

Influencing others

The whole brain model can sometimes help you to influence your counterpart negotiators. For example, if you believe that your counterpart's strength is in the feeling self (quadrant C) and their weakness is in the rational self (quadrant A), you will be more successful if you connect to him or her emotionally by building the relationship, and not by trying to connect cognitively through long speeches or rational arguments.

The four types of thinking styles

A
THE RATIONAL SELF
Individuals with brain dominance in quadrant A tend to be logical, analytical, fact-oriented, and good with numbers.

B
THE SAFEKEEPING SELF
Individuals with brain dominance in quadrant B tend to be cautious, organized, systematic, neat, timely, well-planned, obedient, and risk-averse.

C
THE FEELING SELF
Individuals with brain dominance in quadrant C tend to be friendly, enjoy human interactions, engage in open communication, express their emotions, enjoy teaching, and are supportive of others.

D
THE EXPERIMENTAL SELF
Individuals with brain dominance in quadrant D tend to think holistically and see the big picture. They are also often creative, comfortable with uncertainty, future-oriented, and willing to take risks.

Creating win–win deals

Some negotiators talk about wanting to create win–win deals, but when they hit major roadblocks leave the negotiating table prematurely, thus missing out on an opportunity to make a good deal. Effective negotiators utilize techniques to ensure they can create win–win deals.

SHOW THE WAY
If you are dealing with a win–lose negotiator who thinks that the idea of win–win deals is naive and unrealistic, show them how to create value and reach superior agreements by focusing on interests and bundling issues together.

Getting the conditions right

Effective negotiations, unlike competitive sports, can produce more than one winner. However, it takes motivation by both parties to find creative alternatives that fulfill their interests to create a win–win outcome. To promote win–win deals, effective negotiators focus on both the substantive issues of the deal (price, terms of payment, quality, and delivery schedule) and on formulating a social contract between the negotiators—the spirit of the deal. This involves setting appropriate expectations of how the deal will be negotiated, implemented, and re-visited, in case future disputes arise. If, by contrast, negotiators believe that negotiations are a zero-sum game that must inevitably be won at the expense of the other party, a win–win deal is not possible.

Bundling the issues

Effective negotiators do not negotiate a single issue at a time because this implies that there is a fixed pie and only leads to a win–lose scenario. Instead, they bundle several issues together. Trade-offs can then be made between negotiators because negotiators do not place equal importance on every issue. The principle of bundling issues involves placing an issue that is of high value to you (for example, price) with another that you consider to be of low value (for example, warranty). When you trade-off on issues, you can then keep your high-value issue (price) and give your low-value issue (warranty) away to the other party. The other party, in return, will allow you to have your high-value issue, because your low-value issue is, in fact, of a high value to them. If your low-value issue is also considered to be a low-value issue by the other party, then they will reject the trade-off. Therefore, it is important for you to know what the other party considers to be their high-value issues.

Capitalizing on risk

You can also capitalize on differences in risk tolerance. Some negotiators are more comfortable with high-risk situations than others. As a win–win and risk-taking negotiator, it is possible for you to design a deal where you assume more risk and receive more benefits while your counterpart, who is also a win–win negotiator but risk-averse (avoider), assumes a lower level of risk but receives fewer benefits from the deal.

WIN–WIN NEGOTIATING

FAST TRACK	OFF TRACK
Negotiating on multiple issues simultaneously	Negotiating on only one issue at a time
Understanding what is important to the other party	Focusing exclusively on your own interests
Identifying and leveraging differences in the interests of and the risks to the other party	Ignoring differences in your counterpart's interests and risks

Building relationships

Contract negotiators are typically task-oriented and pragmatic, tend to focus on negotiating specific issues, and do not invest in building relationships. Relationship negotiators, in contrast, invest first in building good relationships before negotiating on specific issues. Effective negotiators need to be skilled at both approaches.

Making a personal connection

Today, more and more Western negotiators value what the Asian, Arabian, and Latin societies recognized thousands of years ago—the value of good relationships. Experienced negotiators invest in building relationships because good relationships "oil" the negotiation process and make it more efficient. For example, Former US Secretary of State James Baker has stated that he has seen this occur time and again—that once negotiators have a good relationship, even the most difficult and conflict-inducing issues have been resolved, simply because the negotiators were more transparent and flexible with each other.

Making contact

Effective negotiators know that, in the long run, good relationships are best built through face-to-face interaction rather than by talking on the telephone or corresponding via email. Where possible, try to create opportunities to socialize with the other party before the negotiations begin. This is not to talk about the negotiations and "discover secrets," but rather to get to know the other person better and connect with them on a human level. The atmosphere of the negotiation process may be very different if you are not meeting your counterpart for the first time at the negotiation table.

CASE STUDY

Being prepared

When US businessman Robert Johnson was looking for investment to enable him to create a new cable channel, Black Entertainment Television, he did his homework. Before pitching the idea to John C. Malone—one of the industry's biggest players—he learned about Malone's business philosophy of believing in the entrepreneurial spirit and of individuals helping themselves rather than relying on others. When they met, Johnson was able to connect with Malone by highlighting their shared business values. This similarity provided a positive start for their successful business negotiations.

Interacting informally

In your interactions with the other party, take advantage of any opportunities to genuinely express your appreciation and congratulate them for their achievements. Use small talk and humor where appropriate—taking opportunities to interact informally will help you build a relationship. Be cautious, however, and use "safe humor" in order not to risk offending the other party. Where possible, focus on the common ground between you. You may find that similarities are personal (the same hobby, for example) or ideological, such as a similar business philosophy. Such findings offer a solid start for building a long-lasting, friendly, and constructive relationship.

Thinking long-term

You should also protect the "face," or dignity, of others and treat them with respect when you are taking more from a deal than they are. This is especially helpful when you are trying to build long-term relationships. In team negotiations, it can work well to include socially skilled negotiators in your team who can take greater responsibility for building lasting relationships, while others (contract negotiators) focus more on the specific issues.

Developing mutual trust

Trust is an essential component of success in all types of negotiation, whether business, diplomatic, or legal. Ambassador Dennis Ross, former US Coordinator of the Middle East, has stated that the ability of negotiators to develop mutual trust is the most important ingredient of successful negotiation, and that without it, negotiations fail.

TREAD CAREFULLY
Although there are many benefits to a trusting relationship, it is not always possible to build trust. Some individuals and groups are simply untrustworthy, so be cautious in your efforts to develop trust.

Understanding the benefits

Trust involves a willingness to take risks. It has to do with how vulnerable one is willing to make oneself to a counterpart. There are many benefits to having trust between negotiators: it promotes openness and transparency, and makes the negotiators more flexible. Negotiators who trust each other take each other's words at face value and do not have to verify their statements. This reduces emotional stress and other transaction costs, and makes the negotiation process more efficient. The likelihood of achieving good and lasting agreements is also higher.

Keeping your commitments

Building trust is difficult but losing it is easy, especially if you break your commitments. The French diplomat Francois de Callier, who wrote the first negotiation book in 1716, stated that a relationship that begins with commitments that cannot be maintained is doomed. Shimon Peres, the President of Israel, has said that promises have to be delivered, otherwise one's reputation is at stake. Although people do sometimes make genuine mistakes and promises in good faith that they ultimately cannot keep, if you want to build trust, you need to make every effort to keep your commitments.

Building your reputation

One of the most important currencies negotiators have is their reputation. It may sometimes be tempting to maximize short-term gains by overlooking the long-term consequences, but experienced negotiators know that people prefer to do business with those that they trust, and guard their reputation fiercely.

Developing trust

Reciprocation is important for building trust. When negotiators offer information or concessions, they expect the other party to reciprocate. Without reciprocation, no further gestures of goodwill will be offered. With reciprocation, the negotiating parties will be able to find ways to collaborate and create value for both.

It is also important to be seen to be fair. As fairness is a subjective matter, however, make sure that you understand the standard of fairness that your counterpart adheres to. Past behavior is often used as a predictor for future behavior, so try to behave consistently.

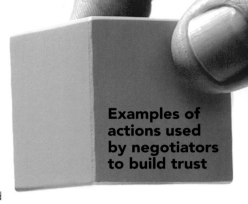

Examples of actions used by negotiators to build trust

When Henry Hollis sold the Palmer House in Chicago to Conrad Hilton, he shook hands on Hilton's first offer of $19,385,000. Within a week Hollis received several offers more than a million dollars higher. However, he never wavered on his first commitment.

In 1873, US financial markets were in poor shape and "king of steel" Andrew Carnegie needed to cash in a $50,000 investment with J.P. Morgan. Expecting a $10,000 profit, he asked Morgan to send him $60,000. Morgan sent $70,000—the investment had made $20,000 profit.

Negotiating fairly

Fairness is an important characteristic in negotiations. Negotiators need to believe that the negotiation process and its outcomes are fair, otherwise they may choose to end the negotiations without coming to an agreement, or fail to put the agreement into action.

Ensuring fairness

There are several categories of fairness that contribute to successful negotiations. Distributive fairness relates to the distribution of outcomes (the splitting of the pie). Negotiators use three different principles of distributive fairness:
• Equality: this states that fairness is achieved by splitting the pie equally.
• Equity: this states that the outcome should relate to the contribution made by each party.
• Needs: this states that, regardless of their contribution, each party should get what they need.

In addition, a negotiator's level of satisfaction and willingness to follow through with an agreement are determined by their perception of the fairness of the procedure (procedural fairness), and also the way they feel they have been treated by the other party (interactional fairness).

Fairness is a subjective issue. When negotiating, if you first define what you consider to be fair, you can then use this "fairness frame" as a bargaining strategy in your discussions with the other party. Alternatively, if you state the importance of fairness at the beginning of the negotiation process, it may encourage the other party to be fair.

CLARITY
Be certain that the final decision is clear, without any potential misinterpretations.

JUSTIFIABILITY
Make sure that all parties are able to explain why you are slicing the pie this way to somebody else.

Ways to ensure that the pie is sliced fairly

SIMPLICITY
Ensure that all negotiating parties can understand and describe the pie-slicing procedures you use to guarantee smooth implementation.

CONSENSUS
Confirm that all parties in the negotiation are in complete agreement on the method of slicing the pie.

CONSISTENCY
Make sure that you apply the fairness principles (equality, equity, or needs) in the same manner throughout the negotiation process.

SATISFACTION
Make sure that all parties are happy with the results—they are then more likely to follow through with the agreement.

Chapter 3
Conducting negotiations

The negotiation process is a strategic interplay between the parties on either side of the table. To be successful, you need to know how to build a strong position, influence your counterpart, deal with difficult situations, and close your deals.

Negotiating with power

Power is a central factor in determining the outcomes of the negotiation process. Effective negotiators understand that power is not static and thus engage in continuously assessing and enhancing it. However, it is equally vital to know how to negotiate when you do not have power.

Understanding power sources

Power can come from a number of different sources:
- **Information** Being well informed enables you to support your arguments and challenge the other party's arguments.
- **BATNA** Having an attractive alternative to a negotiated agreement gives you the power to say "no" to a bad deal and walk away from it.
- **Resources** The party that has more resources—financial, technological, or human—has more power.
- **Needing the deal** The less badly you need the deal, the more power you have not to settle for it.

• **Time** The fewer deadlines you are pressed with, the more power you have to wait and explore opportunities for better deals.
• **Sunk costs** The more willing you are to let go of your sunk costs (such as financial and emotional expenses), the more power you have.
• **Skills** The more skilled you are in the art of negotiation, the more power you have to produce better joint outcomes.

RECOGNIZE YOUR TRUE POWER

Weak parties often underestimate their own power and overestimate that of powerful parties, so try to make an objective assessment of the amount of power you have.

Negotiating from a weak position

If your position is weak, never share this information with the other party. New information or opportunities may arise at any point, which may strengthen your BATNA and your negotiating position. Even if your position is weak overall, try to identify any areas of strength you have and use them as leverage. Even the most powerful party will have some weaknesses, so try to discover these and target them.

Never make "all or nothing" deals from a weak position—you may miss out on opportunities that would have arisen as the value of what you are bringing to the table increases during the negotiation process. Instead, make deals sequentially and in small chunks, to ensure that the other party will be more likely to recognize the added value that you bring to the table.

USE LIKEABILITY AND INTEGRITY

When in a weak position, do not underestimate the power of personal likeability. People do business with people they like and whom they can trust to keep their promises and deliver good value.

CASE STUDY

Creating power

When Thomas Stemberg, the founder of office products retailer Staples, needed a new round of capital to expand his business, he went back to the venture capitalists who had already financed the company. This time, however, they closed ranks and demanded a higher equity share than Stemberg was willing to provide. Determined to break the venture capitalists' cartel, Stemberg sought alternative sources of funding—the pension funds, the insurance companies, and high net worth individuals—with which he could negotiate from a more powerful position.

Making offers and counteroffers

Before you go into a negotiation, it is vital to plan your opening move. Do you open negotiations and make the first offer or do you wait and allow the other party to go first? Make sure that you have an opening offer in mind, and plan how you will respond to your counterpart's offers.

Knowing when to go first

Some experts suggest that you should not make the first offer and should always allow your counterpart to go first. Skilled negotiators, however, question the conventional "never open" rule. They choose to tailor their approach to each negotiation. How should you decide whether to go first or second? You should present your offer first when you are confident in the thoroughness of your due diligence and also when you suspect that your counterpart is ill-informed. By going first, you will "anchor," or set a benchmark, that will be used as a reference point for the counteroffer.

If you are not fully informed, do not go first. Consider the other party's first offer, do not respond to it, and do your due diligence. In some cases, two negotiators are equally skilled and well informed and neither wishes to go first. Such cases often require the involvement of a trusted third party to act as a neutral go-between and get the negotiations started.

Setting your offer

Whether you present your offer first or second, how high should your offer be? Former US Secretary of State Dr. Henry Kissinger believes that a negotiator is better off starting with a high offer. Most negotiators, however, tend to negotiate first with themselves and thus restrain themselves from making bold offers. They tend to justify their modest offers by thinking that their counterparts would not go for a higher offer. Experts today suggest that a seller who puts forward a high offer may risk his or her credibility and offend the buyer, who may very well walk away without even providing a counteroffer. Instead of coming up with offers that are either too high or too modest, it is often better to make offers that are bold and daring. Bold and daring offers are reasonably high, tend not to be acceptable, but are still negotiable.

TIP

CONSIDER THE LONGER TERM

If you are hoping to form a long-term relationship with the other party, do not take advantage if they make you a very low first offer. You will generate goodwill and nurture the relationship if you instead respond with a counteroffer that is higher, but still reasonable to you.

🔍 IN FOCUS... POSSIBLE RESPONSES TO TOUGH OPENING OFFERS

It is easy to be thrown if the other party's opening offer is extremely low. Effective negotiators make sure that they are not startled by a tough first offer, and avoid making a quick, emotional reaction. It is vital that a low opening offer does not become a benchmark for the negotiation. Possible responses to low offers include rejecting the offer as unreasonable; asking the other party to revise the offer; or asking questions and probing the other party for justifications for the toughness of the offer.

Making concessions

Experienced negotiators know that successful negotiations involve a certain amount of give and take, and are well versed in the process of making concessions. They tend to develop offers that leave room for concessions, as these are the oil that lubricates the making of a deal.

Conceding in small steps

Each negotiation event is unique, so there are no absolute rules for how to make concessions that apply to all situations. However, it is generally true that people like to receive good news or benefits in installments, rather than all at once. Skilled negotiators, therefore, tend to make multiple small concessions in order to increase the level of satisfaction of their counterpart.

Knowing what to concede

WATCH YOUR TIMING

Think carefully about the timing of your first sizeable concession. If you make it too soon after your initial offer, it will give the other party the impression that the initial offer was not a credible one.

Inexperienced negotiators often make a first sizeable concession as an expression of goodwill. However, this can set the expectation that there are many concessions to be provided. Experienced negotiators, by contrast, tend to untangle the relationships from the concessions. Sometimes, in order to set the tone of reciprocating concessions, they concede first by making a concession on a minor issue.

Wait before you make the first sizeable concession. During this time, advocate for your initial offer and convey the idea that it is not that easy to make concessions. The second concession should be smaller in size than the first and be a longer time in coming. Making concessions in progressively declining installments will then lend more credibility to when you finally say: "There is no more to give."

Making and interpreting concessions

ENABLING RECIPROCITY
Label the concessions you make as ones that are costly to you and then reduce your value. This sets up the expectation that you will receive a concession in return, implying value for value.

USING CONTINGENCY
If you suspect that your concession will not be reciprocated, offer a concession that is contingent upon the other party providing a concession in return. For example: "I will be willing to extend the terms of payment to 45 days if you will increase your order by 500 items."

SETTING BOUNDARIES
Some negotiators put the deal at risk by asking for too much. Set boundaries for the other party by being clear and precise about what you can concede and what you absolutely cannot.

SETTING RULES
Sometimes negotiators make final concessions but then withdraw them or make them contingent on receiving a new concession. Set a clear rule that a concession cannot be withdrawn, unless it was explicitly offered as a tentative or conditional concession.

SPOTTING DEAL-BREAKERS
Some concessions are deal-breakers: if they are not offered, your counterpart will walk away from the negotiation table. Try to distinguish these from value-enhancing concessions, which are demands that are designed to get a better deal, but if not provided, would not result in the other party abandoning the negotiations.

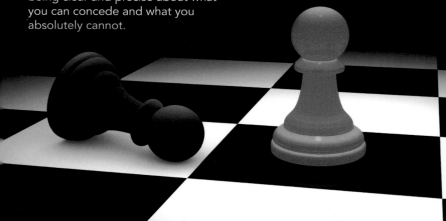

Being persuasive

A successful negotiation process requires effective persuasion. When attempting to influence your counterpart, it is crucial to identify your moments of power and take advantage of them. Seasoned negotiators understand how to use appropriate persuasion techniques to sell their ideas to the other party.

Influencing others

Effective negotiators use a range of influencing techniques that take advantage of the natural responses of negotiators to certain types of information. For example, negotiators are generally more motivated to avoid losses than they are to obtain gains. A group of home-owners in California was given the advice that "if you insulate your home, you will gain 50 cents a day". Another group was told that "if you fail to insulate your home, you will lose 50 cents a day." More home owners under the second set of instructions insulated their homes than under the first set of instructions. Similarly, you are more likely to persuade the other party of the benefits of your deal if you emphasize what they would lose if they don't agree, not what they could gain if they do.

Making small unilateral concessions can be a successful way to influence your counterpart. Negotiators feel obligated to reciprocate, no matter how big or small the concessions are. Even a small concession on your part can help the other party to comply. The more beneficial your concession is to the other side, the more likely they are to feel obliged to return the favor.

USE SCARCITY
It is human nature for people to want more of what they cannot have. When you present your offer to the other party, inform them of the unique benefits you are offering that they would not be able to get elsewhere.

GAIN COMMITMENT
Encourage the other party to agree to an initially modest request. They are then more likely to follow up with their commitment by agreeing to your key demand to justify their past decision to say yes to you.

Strengthening your hand with persuasion techniques

GIVE "SOCIAL PROOF"
People often use "social proof" when making decisions—they think that if many people are doing things a certain way, it must be good. Demonstrate how your product or service has been successfully used by others.

LET THEM SAY "NO"
Give the other party the opportunity to say "no" by making an outrageous demand, before retreating immediately and putting forward a reasonable demand. This can also serve to make the other party feel obligated to make a concession.

GIVE A REASON
People are much more likely to agree to a demand if you have given legitimate justification for it. Try to give a reason that can be backed up with evidence, but using even a frivolous reason increases your chances of reaching agreement.

SET A BENCHMARK
Negotiators who are not fully informed tend to compare the cost of an item to a reference point or benchmark. You can influence the way they make their decision by setting a benchmark for them.

Managing impasses

Negotiations do not always conclude with an agreement. You may encounter an impasse or a deadlock during the process. How should you deal with a deadlock? Should you leave the negotiation table, concluding that the process has failed, or should you encourage yourself and your counterpart to remain at the table and keep the negotiations going?

Dealing with deadlock

Skilled and experienced negotiators expect there to be impasses in the negotiating process. They anticipate deadlocks and develop counteractions to deal with them when they occur. They view an impasse as a natural ingredient in negotiations and do not give up easily in their attempts to reach an agreement.

Impasses usually generate negative emotions and sometimes deep feelings of resentment. Prior to and during the negotiation process, you have to be sensitive to the other party's concerns, feelings, and, particularly, their self-image. Research has suggested that negotiators have an image to uphold and that negotiations are less likely to be successful when either or both parties are not sensitive enough to each other's dignity, or "face." You should always be mindful not to harm the self-image of your counterpart, and never more so than during critical moments of an impasse.

Oiling the wheels

If you are facing an impasse, experts suggest that, in the intensity of the moment, you should first take time out to cool down. This will help to defuse the emotional situation and you can resume the discussion at a later time.

Once you reconvene, start by trying to highlight any existing mutual benefits. Impasses usually occur after some progress has already been made. It can therefore be useful to frame the impasse in the context of what has already been achieved—the gains—and highlight the potential losses to both parties if agreement is not reached.

If you are still deadlocked, you may need to try expanding the pie. If you maintain a zero-sum, fixed-pie mentality toward the negotiation, this will restrain your creativity in negotiating for the best deal. Consider that the purpose of negotiation is not to win an argument, but to find satisfactory solutions that would maximize the benefits for both parties. Take time to generate possible new ideas that could help you reach agreement. Expand the issues you are discussing, but avoid making concessions. In this way, you may be able to overcome the impasse on one critical issue by adding another issue that is attractive to the other party.

MANAGING DEADLOCK SITUATIONS

FAST TRACK	**OFF TRACK**
Anticipating potential impasses and planning in advance how to deal with them	Believing that you can just think on your feet if a problem arises
Being open-minded and flexible, and finding creative solutions	Thinking that deadlocks always lead to "no deal"
Reacting calmly and using your emotional intelligence, because you know that deadlock situations can be resolved	Leaving the negotiating table early because you are deadlocked with the other party

Avoiding decision traps

Most negotiators believe that they are rational. In reality, many negotiators systematically make errors of judgment and irrational choices. It is important for you to understand and try to avoid making these common errors, as they lead to poor decision-making.

TIP

WATCH YOUR TIMING

To avoid feeling that you have not made the best possible deal, never accept the first offer, even when it is a great offer. Always negotiate a little.

Making the right decisions

Understanding the decision traps that negotiators can fall into will help you avoid making the same mistakes yourself, and may allow you to use the other party's errors to leverage your own power. To avoid decision traps or to use them to your advantage:

• Do not hesitate to reverse your original decision and cut your losses; create an exit strategy even before you get involved in the negotiation process.

• Take the opportunity to set a benchmark that could give you an advantage when your counterpart is ill-informed, but be aware that they could do the same to you if you yourself are not fully informed.

• Engage a trusted expert who will challenge your overconfidence in your ability to negotiate and put pressure on you to do a reality check.

• Make sure that your offer is based on solid research. When buying, equip yourself with some security by demanding a performance guarantee of the product.

• Invest time and energy in looking for information that is not easily available. You will often find accessible information that can improve your position.

• Present information more or less vividly to influence others, but be wary of overvaluing information that is attractively presented to you.

• As a negotiator, be aware of how the other party frames the situation and presents its offers.

• Approach each negotiating event as a unique case. They are never identical.

UNDERSTANDING DECISION ERRORS

ERROR	DESCRIPTION
Non-rational escalation of commitment	• Acting contrary to your self-interest by increasing your commitment to an original decision, despite the fact that this decision produces negative outcomes ("throwing good money after bad").
Anchoring and adjustment	• Using a faulty anchor as a benchmark from which to make adjustments and decisions. An ill-informed home-buyer, for example, may use the seller's asking price as an anchor for their counteroffer, rather than solid due diligence on home values.
Overconfidence	• Believing that you are more correct and accurate than you actually are. This leads to an overestimation of your power within the negotiation, the options open to you, and the probability of your success.
The winner's curse	• If you settle quickly on a deal when selling, feeling that the "win" was too easy and that you could have got more from the deal. • If you settle quickly on a deal when buying, thinking "I could have got this for less" or "What is wrong with this item? I must have got a bad deal."
Information availability bias	• Making a decision based on limited information, even though information is readily available or would have been available if enough effort had been put in to finding it.
Vividness bias	• Recalling and assigning more weight to information that was delivered in a vivid fashion, and giving less weight to equally important, but dull, information.
Framing and risk	• Making decisions based on how the issues were framed (for example, a glass may be described as being half empty or half full). Risk-averse negotiators are more likely to respond positively to offers that are framed in terms of losses, for example, because they are afraid of losing out; risk-seeking negotiators, by contrast, will respond slowly, because they are willing to wait for a better offer.
Small numbers bias	• Drawing a conclusion based on a small number of events, cases, or experiences, believing that your limited experience allows you to generalize from it.

Managing emotions

In the heat of a negotiation, the emotions you display can significantly influence the emotions of the other party. Effective negotiators try to synchronize their behavior with the other person's, developing an interpersonal rhythm that reflects a shared emotional state.

Understanding the approaches

There are three types of emotional approach in negotiations: rational (having a "poker face"), positive (being friendly and nice), and negative (ranting and raving). Some negotiators believe that exposing their emotions to the other party makes them vulnerable and will result in them giving away too much of the pie, and so try to always keep a "poker face" when they are negotiating. They also believe that emotional displays may result in an impasse or in defective decision-making, or cause negotiations to end.

Other negotiators believe that displaying positive emotions enhances the quality of the negotiated agreement, because a good mood promotes creative thinking, leads to innovative problem-solving, and smoothes out communication. Negotiators with a positive approach use more cooperative strategies, engage in more information exchange, generate more alternatives, use fewer hard tactics, and come to fewer impasses than negotiators with a negative or rational mood.

Q IN FOCUS...
STRATEGIC USE OF ANGER

Some negotiators successfully use displays of anger strategically to try to encourage the other party to agree to their demands. They aim to gain concessions from their opponent because the other party takes their anger as a sign that they are close to their reservation point. Inducing fear in their opponent pushes that person to cave in and agree. It sends the signal that they would rather walk away from the table without reaching an agreement than settle for less than what they want. The opponent may also wish to end the unpleasant interaction sooner by giving in.

Being negative

Negotiators who use the negative approach display anger, rage, and impatience in order to influence the other party. Anger is sometimes used strategically, but negotiators who are genuinely angry feel little compassion for the other party, and are less effective at expanding and slicing the pie than positive negotiators. They tend to achieve fewer win–win gains when angry than when they experience positive emotions. Angry negotiators are also less willing to cooperate and more likely to seek revenge.

Of the three emotional strategies, the positive and rational approaches are more effective than the negative approach in achieving targets in an ultimatum setting. The positive approach is more helpful in building a long-term, constructive relationship than the rational or negative methods.

Using emotional intelligence

When negotiators are emotionally overwhelmed, their mental capacity to negotiate effectively is impaired. To overcome this, you must manage your emotions intelligently. You need to be aware of the emotions you are experiencing and be able to monitor and regulate them, and you need to find ways to empathize with the other party. For example, when the US Secretary of State James Baker was negotiating with Hafez al-Assad, President of Syria, he had to make a conscious attempt to modulate his irritation. Although he was very angry when President Assad retracted from an earlier commitment, he used the term "misunderstanding" rather than openly displaying his anger.

ASK YOURSELF... DO I USE EMOTIONAL INTELLIGENCE WHEN NEGOTIATING?

- Am I able to make an emotional connection with my counterpart, even if I do not know them very well?
- Am I able to judge when my own emotions threaten to affect my ability to make rational decisions?
- Can I manage my emotions to ensure that I am always effective?
- Am I able to react in a measured way, keeping my emotions under control, even if the other party is using value-claiming tactics or behaving in a manner that I do not agree with?

Dealing with competitive tactics

In competitive win–lose position-based negotiations, negotiators use various manipulative tactics to maximize their interests while disregarding the interests of their counterparts. They usually believe that these tactics are quite effective. Often, however, these tactics can backfire, escalating the level of negotiation or even leading to an impasse. Skilled negotiators recognize these tactical traps and know how to avoid and neutralize them.

Competitive tactics and how to avoid them

MAKING A HIGHBALL OR LOWBALL OFFER
A negotiator assumes that you are not fully informed and tries to take advantage by making a very high offer as a seller, or a low offer as a buyer. Their objective is to replace the benchmark you have in your mind with one in their favor.
TO AVOID: Be confident in your benchmarks and try to see clearly through this ploy.

PLAYING GOOD GUY/BAD GUY
One negotiator plays tough and uses aggressive tactics, such as threats and ultimatums. Another empathizes to make you believe that he or she is on your side. Neither is on your side—both are trying to maximize their own interests.
TO AVOID: Focus squarely on protecting your own interests.

SEPARATING THE ISSUES

A negotiator insists on reaching an agreement on a single issue before moving on to the next issue. This prevents you from bundling issues together and creating opportunities for trade-offs.
TO AVOID: Negotiate multiple issues at once, stating that "nothing is agreed upon until everything is agreed upon."

NIBBLING

The deal is done, but at the last minute the negotiator asks for another small concession. Most negotiators concede, fearing that the last-minute demand might derail the deal if it is not fulfilled.
TO AVOID: Remember that refusing to budge on a small concession at the last minute is not usually a deal-breaker.

APPLYING TIME PRESSURE

The other party uses the pressure of time to try to get you to concede by setting tight deadlines for an offer, or using delaying tactics to reduce the amount of time available for the negotiation.
TO AVOID: Use your judgement to decide whether a deadline is real or not.

USING EMOTIONAL BLACKMAIL

A negotiator tries to intimidate or influence you by fabricating anger, frustration, or despair. They try to emotionally shake you and make you feel responsible for the lack of progress.
TO AVOID: Use your emotional intelligence. Stay calm and centered, and try to steer the negotiations back on track.

Closing the deal

Closing the deal after reaching an agreement is the last but most critical part of any negotiation process. It is certainly not simple, and is not just about outcomes. It also has to do with building relationships and making sure that the negotiated agreements can be carried out smoothly. Closing the deal properly is especially important when negotiated agreements are complex and multi-dimensional.

Preparing to close

Before you close the deal, both you and your counterpart need to understand that the purpose of making the deal is not to sign the contract, but rather to accomplish what the contract specifies. What goals is each party pursuing through the deal and what will it take to accomplish them? As you depend on each other to accomplish your goals, it is important to make sure that both parties are signing the contract wholeheartedly. Review both parties' key interests and ensure that nothing has been neglected. It is quite possible for the other party to decide to overturn the entire deal if he or she feels pushed into an agreement without having their own needs taken care of.

✔ CHECKLIST **CLOSING A DEAL**

	YES	NO
• Have you considered all possible stakeholders?	☐	☐
• Have you clarified the purpose of the deal?	☐	☐
• Have you made sure that both parties understand what it takes to implement the agreement?	☐	☐
• Have you built a relationship with the other party, to pave the way for future collaboration?	☐	☐
• Have you made enough arrangements for another team to implement the agreement, if another team is taking over?	☐	☐

Considering implementation

Most negotiators underestimate the importance of implementation. If not considered, the intense process of negotiation can undermine your ability to achieve your goals after the deal has been signed. For example, if you have used hard negotiation tactics to push the other party to agree to the deal, the other party may feel, upon signing the contract, that they have been unfairly treated and sabotage the deal, or fail to deliver.

Before you put pen to paper, discuss the implementation of the deal with the other party. What you agree must fulfill the needs of both parties if you are to ensure successful implementation. Unless both parties have confidence that the deal can be successfully implemented, there is no point in continuing the discussion.

Reaching agreement

A written agreement usually marks the closure of a negotiation. The agreement, which includes solutions for both parties, may be summarized and you may ask the other party to sign this document. This is the most simple and natural way to conclude a negotiation.

HOW TO...
ENSURE EFFECTIVE IMPLEMENTATION

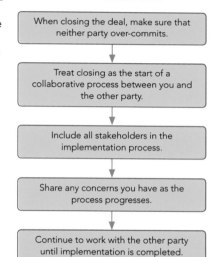

When closing the deal, make sure that neither party over-commits.

Treat closing as the start of a collaborative process between you and the other party.

Include all stakeholders in the implementation process.

Share any concerns you have as the process progresses.

Continue to work with the other party until implementation is completed.

Changes should be allowed after the agreement has been signed. In other words, if circumstances change, both parties should feel comfortable contacting the other party to discuss these changes. Upon mutual agreement, such changes can be incorporated into the new agreement. Make sure you include this last point in the agreement, as a deal is not done until it is done—it is better to allow for some flexibility than to force the other party to overthrow the entire deal, should the circumstances change.

Chapter 4

Developing your technique

However experienced you are at negotiating, there are always ways to improve your technique. Negotiating in groups, in an international arena, and using your skills to mediate conflicts all require a tailored approach to achieve the best results.

Negotiating as a team

Many business situations are too complex for a solo negotiator to be fully informed about every aspect of the deal. In such cases, working in a team may give better results, though this requires a high degree of internal coordination and a smooth flow of information between members.

Deciding when to use a team

Some negotiations demand a diverse set of abilities. In addition to sound negotiation and psychosocial skills you may need specific technical expertise, for example, in areas of law, drafting joint ventures, or the planning system. You may need to exercise leverage on your opposite number through the use of PR, or require a keen appreciation of strategy and politics in order to identify the multiple stakeholders in the negotiation and figure out their interests. If you lack any of these abilities, you will probably benefit from the collective wisdom of a team.

Understanding the advantages

There are many benefits to negotiating as a team. Being part of a team provides for multiple creative trade-offs and options and has other advantages, too. Sheer "strength in numbers" makes a team feel secure and powerful and sends a clear message to the other party that you are serious about the deal. You are also likely to feel less pressured when negotiating as a team, and are unlikely to make too many concessions too early in the process.

TIP

MAKE TIME TO PREPARE

Make sure that you have enough time to create a cohesive, trustworthy team, and allow time to prepare your strategy as a group before you enter into a team negotiation.

Avoiding the pitfalls

Working in a team can lead to a lack of focus and consistency, so appoint a chief negotiator to lead your team and agree in advance each member's roles and responsibilities. Avoid falling into "groupthink," when team members feel pressured to conform to an existing group mindset and reluctant to present ideas that conflict with it. It can also be easy for a team to create a false sense of cohesiveness: "us," the good team, versus "them," the bad team. If this happens, genuine conciliatory attempts made by the other party can be dismissed as dishonest "tricks" and rejected, resulting in missed opportunities to make a deal.

 IN FOCUS... DECISION TIME

Negotiating as a team begs the question of how to decide on a course of action. Broadly, there are three ways to reach a decision: first is unanimity, in which all team members must agree on a given issue. This is a tough rule and not recommended for most situations. Second is the majority rule. The majority will decide and the minority comply with the decision. The hazard here is that the majority may impose a tough solution that the minority cannot live with. The third, and usually best, decision-making rule is consensus: making a decision that not all the team members agree with fully, but that all can live with.

Dealing with many parties

Many business partnerships or deals involve agreements between three or more different parties, each with their own positions, needs, and goals. Negotiating in this environment requires dexterity and a constant eye on the pitfalls, such as coalitions between the parties opposing you.

Balancing complex issues

Multiparty negotiations are in many ways similar to two-party situations but require a wider set of skills to deal with their additional complexities, which include:

• **Informational complexity** The number of parties involved produces multiple exchanges of information, proposals, and multiple trade-offs. You need to develop a solid information system that can record and recall all the information exchanged in the negotiation room.

• **Strategic complexity** Multiple parties have many interests, and often conflicts of interest, between them. Each party has its BATNA (Best Alternative to a Negotiated Agreement), which may change as alliances are formed. To be well prepared for a multiparty negotiation, you must constantly reassess your own and your counterparts' BATNAs.

CASE STUDY

Chairing multiparty talks

The central challenge for the Chair of a meeting is to gain the trust of the negotiating parties. Former Senator George J. Mitchell, US Senate Majority Leader, stated that in mediating the dispute in Northern Ireland, his ability to be effective ultimately depended more on gaining the delegates' trust and confidence than on his formal role and authority. The Chair should be clear about his or her role, introduce the agenda, introduce ground rules, provide parties with opportunities to express themselves, and distil common interests. The Chair should also regularly summarize the progress that has been made in the negotiation.

SUCCEEDING IN MULTIPARTY NEGOTIATIONS

FAST TRACK

OFF TRACK

FAST TRACK	OFF TRACK
Forming or joining coalitions	Insisting on acting independently
Resisting group pressure to modify your core interests	Settling too easily when faced by a coalition
Being clear when you disagree	Keeping quiet: silence may be interpreted as assent
Monitoring the positions of all the parties	Focusing on only one part of the negotiations

• **Procedural complexity** The design of the negotiation process may be fraught with difficulty. Its structure—the rules of engagement, the selection of the venue, the sequence of the issues, and how decisions will be made—must be perceived by all parties to be fair. In high-value negotiations, it is wise to employ a trained expert to facilitate the process more effectively.

• **Social complexity** With more negotiators involved, the social context becomes complex. In a two-party negotiation, your focus is on one individual, but multiparty negotiations require you to understand, analyze, and build relationships with each and every negotiator. You must learn to resist excessive social pressure and always protect your interests, even when faced by a coalition of parties in the negotiation.

• **Emotional complexity** Negotiating in a multiparty context can be very taxing. Make sure that your emotions are held in check; emotional distress often results in poor decisions.

TIP

GAIN POWER
Consider building a coalition if you think you hold a weaker hand than one of your opponents. Being part of a successful coalition may help you shift the balance of power.

Building winning coalitions

The moment there are more than two parties in a negotiation, there are opportunities to make coalitions. To protect your interests and remain in the negotiating game, one of your major objectives is to think well in advance about offence (how to build a winning coalition) as well as defence (how to put together a blocking coalition).

When attempting to build a stable coalition, there are three essential factors to consider. The first is the issue of agreement. Some parties will agree and others will disagree with your vision and the strategies and tactics you plan to use to achieve it. The second is influence. Some potential partners may be highly influential and can use their positions of power to assist you in moving your agenda forward, while others will be weak and unable to help much. The third factor to consider is trust. Coalitions are temporary entities driven by self-interest, so partners are easily seduced to defect once the pay-offs elsewhere become higher. Your main objective should be to recruit potential partners who are trustworthy and will remain loyal to the coalition.

TIP

DIVIDE THE PIE
Make it clear to your coalition partners how the benefits—the proverbial pie—will be divided if you achieve your goals. The division certainly must be fair, but fairness does not necessarily mean an equal share.

? ASK YOURSELF... ABOUT FORMING A COALITION

- What is your agenda for the negotiation and what are you trying to achieve?
- What are the main factors that you need to consider in building your coalition?
- Can you identify potential coalition partners that are most likely to work with you to allow you to jointly fulfill your objectives?
- How should you sequence the recruitment of each potential coalition partner?
- What is the best way to approach potential partners?

Recruiting coalition partners

When building a coalition, start by identifying all stakeholders, both supporters and opponents of your objectives. Classify each one according to their level of agreement (high, medium, or low, on a scale from one to 10), the degree of influence they could bring to the coalition, and their level of perceived trustworthiness. First, approach your best potential allies—the parties who agree with your vision and agenda and are very influential and trustworthy. Next, focus on the allies who agree with your vision and are trustworthy, but who do not hold positions of power at the moment; they may gain influence as the negotiation proceeds. Ignore the weak adversaries: those who disagree with your agenda and have little influence. At the same time, think how you could block your powerful adversaries. Can you make a coalition with one of their potential partners?

Coalition partners are often motivated solely by gains. Once the gains elsewhere are higher, they may defect, so you should attempt to cement integrity within the coalition. One way to do this is to ask each partner to make a public commitment to the coalition, making it harder for them to defect.

Negotiating internationally

In today's global economy, ever more business deals are made across national borders. Negotiating international deals is a considerable challenge because you must be familiar with the complexities of the immediate negotiation context, such as the bargaining power of the parties and the relevant stakeholders, as well as the broader context, which may include currency fluctuations and government control.

Understanding the differences

You are likely to experience significant differences in several key areas when you engage in international negotiation:

• **Agreements** Western negotiators expect to conclude the process with a comprehensive bullet-proof legal contract. In other countries, and notably in Asia, memorandums of understanding (MOAs), which are broader but less substantial agreements, may be more common.

• **Time sensitivity** In countries in which a "doing" culture is prevalent, people believe in controlling events and managing time strictly. In some countries, time is not viewed as such a critical resource, and negotiations can be slow and lengthy.

• **Degree of formality** Negotiators from informal cultures tend to dress down, address one another by their first names, maintain less physical distance, and pay less attention to official titles. In contrast, negotiators from formal cultures tend to use formal titles and are mindful of seating arrangements.

POLITICAL RISK
While some countries have long traditions of an abundance of resources and political stability, others have scarce resources and are marked by volatile political changes.

IDEOLOGY
In individualistic cultures like the US, the purpose of the business is to serve the interests of its shareholders, but in collective cultures, the business has a larger purpose: to contribute to the common good of society.

POLITICAL AND LEGAL SYSTEMS

Different countries have different tax codes, labor laws, legal philosophies and enforcement policies, laws that govern joint ventures, and financial incentives for attracting business investments.

Factors to consider in international negotiations

BUREAUCRACY

Business practices and government regulations vary from country to country. In some countries, the government bureaucracy is deeply embedded in business affairs, and businesses are constantly required to secure government approval before they act.

INTERNATIONAL FINANCE

Currencies fluctuate and affect the balance of expenses and profits. The stability of the currency your investment is made in affects the risk to you. Many governments also control the flow of currency, limiting the amount of money that can cross their borders.

CULTURE

Different cultures have starkly different cultural beliefs about the role of individuals in society, the nature of relationships, and the ways in which people should communicate. These have a fundamental effect on how you need to approach a negotiation.

Negotiating in Asia

Succeeding in any international negotiation means taking the time to understand the complex negotiating environment, being sufficiently flexible to be able to change your ways if necessary, and learning to work within governmental bureaucracies. The cultural and business landscape in Asia is especially unfamiliar to Western organizations, and, with the region's rapid rise to economic prominence, every manager needs to be aware of how it differs.

Acknowledging differences

Asian culture is characterized by concern for people's feelings. It emphasizes interdependence, harmony, and cooperation, while Western culture tends to be more competitive and achievement-oriented, and rewards assertiveness.

Asian societies give a higher priority to collective goals; self-sacrifice for the good of the whole is a guiding principle. There is a greater acceptance of unequal power distribution, and relationships are built based on differences of stature, age, and gender.

Another cultural differentiator is the level of comfort of individuals in ambiguous situations. Business people in China and Japan like to avoid uncertainty, preferring structured and clear situations, in which they are able to make decisions after careful evaluation of a large amount of information. Contrast this with some Western societies, where people are more comfortable with ambiguous situations and are prepared to make quick decisions based on a limited amount of information.

Be aware too that there are differences in communication styles: Asians may be "high context" (indirect, implicit, and suggestive), while those from the West are "low context"—more direct and specific.

TIP

MAKE A CONNECTION

Present your partners with a long-term vision of the mutual benefits of a deal, stressing your personal relationship rather than legal obligations.

TIP

BE PATIENT

Indian negotiators are more concerned with getting good outcomes than with the efficiency of the negotiation process, and may negotiate for weeks or even months to get the best deal. Never put pressure on your counterpart to reach agreement more quickly or you may lose the deal.

The Asian style of negotiation

RELATIONSHIPS ("GUANXI")
Chinese business leaders invest heavily in making interpersonal connections and creating a dependable social network, known as "guanxi." They prefer to do business within their trusted network.

EMOTIONS
The Confucian teaching *xinping qihe*, meaning "being perfectly calm," makes it difficult for Western negotiators to "read" their counterparts and to know where they stand.

FAIRNESS
The concept of fairness is based on needs: those who have more should give to those with less.

TRUST FROM THE HEART
Asian businesses like to do business with trustworthy individuals rather than faceless organizations. The lengthy process of building trust is based on openness, mutual assistance, understanding, and the formation of emotional bonds.

FACE
Dignity and prestige are gained when individuals behave morally and achieve accomplishments. Face is a formidable force in the Asian psyche that negotiators in Western organizations must be particularly aware of.

LEGALISM
You risk insulting your Asian counterpart if you emphasize penalties for dishonoring commitments in detail. Contracts are short and merely a tangible expression of the relationships being created. They are not treated as "fixed" legal instruments.

DECISIONS
Although Chinese and Japanese societies are hierarchical, they use the consensus style of decision-making. Lead negotiators refrain from dictating a decision in order to preserve relationships and give face to others.

Examining the role of gender

Are women better negotiators than men? Research reveals real differences in negotiation styles between the genders, but there are also deep-seated gender stereotypes in many cultures. How these gender differences are handled, by both men and women, is critical in determining the quality of the agreement you reach through negotiation.

Being aware of perceptions

Enthusiastic and well-prepared negotiators, whether men or women, tend to perform better than less-interested and less-committed ones. In an ideal world, in which neither party is concerned about gender, female negotiators can perform just as well as their male counterparts. In the real world, it pays to be aware of the real and perceived differences between the sexes when approaching a negotiation.

Addressing stereotypes

Women are stereotypically portrayed as being at a disadvantage in the negotiating environment. The myths are that, while men behave rationally, women are emotional; where men are assertive, women are passive; and while men are competitive, women tend to prefer a collaborative approach.

As a woman, your attitude toward these stereotypes and how you choose to handle them when negotiating with men plays a critical role in determining the outcome of a negotiation. If you accept the stereotype and feel and appear anxious at the negotiating table, you may confirm the stereotype and trigger a self-fulfilling prophecy of expecting less and getting less. If you acknowledge the stereotype and try hard to overcome it, you will gain advantage; people are generally prompted to assert their freedom when they feel restricted by others, and using these feelings in a negotiation may serve to make you bolder and more assertive, and help you gain a bargaining surplus.

Men may also be affected by perceived or real gender differences in negotiations. When men negotiate with women, they may either choke under the pressure to over-perform, thus leading to a less favorable outcome; or they may feel guilty and fail to take advantage of their male traits, which would also lead to a less favorable outcome.

GENDER DIFFERENCES IN NEGOTIATION

AREA OF ACTIVITY	MALE CHARACTERISTICS	FEMALE CHARACTERISTICS
Setting goals	Tend to set high goals	Tend to set lower goals
Making concessions	Tend to make few concessions	Tend to make more concessions
Splitting the pie	Focus more on outcomes—getting a larger slice of the pie	Focus more on building and maintaining relationships than obtaining an outcome
Accepting offers	Tend to regret their decision later and feel they could have got more, especially after accepting a first offer	Tend to feel relieved after accepting an offer

Using a coach

Many negotiators have blind spots, hold false assumptions, and are prone to repeating their mistakes. Some continue to fail to fully understand the other party's perspective, are unable to convert positions to interests, or are unable to manage their emotions. Working with a coach is an excellent way to gain perspective on your weaknesses and strengths and develop your skills for greater success.

Understanding the benefits

Many negotiators do not realize that they could improve their techniques. They continue to make the same mistakes because they filter information, hearing only what they want to hear, rather than absorbing the complete information that is required to perform well. Another self-serving trap is attribution. Negotiators often attribute problems in negotiations to their counterpart negotiators. An objective coach who is willing to challenge you can help raise your awareness of your limitations and improve your performance.

DEVELOPING YOUR SKILLS

FAST TRACK	OFF TRACK
Embracing coaching as a way to become more successful	Rejecting an offer of coaching, because you can't improve
Respecting your coach's assessment of your weaknesses	Believing that your coach doesn't understand your superior approach
Using the feedback your coach gives you to improve your skills	Dismissing your coach's advice, because you know better

Working with a coach

When you first work with a coach, they will make an assessment of your performance. This often starts with a 360-degree feedback session, in which your coach collects data from people you negotiate with, in order to identify your strengths and weaknesses. The coach may also "shadow" you in actual negotiations, to take note of your performance. Witnessing you in action allows a coach to provide relevant and insightful suggestions for improvement. The key outcome from the diagnosis is for the coach to identify your patterns in beliefs and behaviors, so that you have a higher level of self-awareness.

Fine-tuning your style

The coach then works with you to identify the skill sets and attitudes you want to focus on throughout the coaching period. Coaches are experienced in diagnosing possible pitfalls in your negotiation styles, and can help you be proactive in preventing them from occurring. They can also help you to uncover issues and resolve them on your own. They can expand your repertoire of behaviors by trying out different approaches and styles with you. Coaches ask

IN FOCUS...
ROLE PLAY

Scenario role play can be an effective method of preparing for negotiations. A coach can help you rehearse your role and make sure there are no gaps or weaknesses in your case and in the negotiation process. For example, the coach can help identify your BATNA or make sure that you are not too enamored with the potential deal to the extent that you are unable to walk away from it. Although it is impossible to perfectly script a negotiation process ahead of time, it is helpful to "know your destination and all the terrain" so that even if the other party takes the process off track, you can still find a way to achieve your goals.

a lot of questions. A good coach helps the negotiator to test his or her own assumptions, consider different perspectives, and reach a conclusion about how to proceed. Many will use scenario role play to help you practice new ways of doing things.

Once you have used the new approaches in a real negotiation, a coach can provide a non-threatening evaluation and help you learn from your mistakes, achievements, and missed opportunities. Your learning can then be applied in your next round of negotiations.

Being a mediator

As a manager, you will often have to negotiate directly with others within your organization, but will also sometimes be asked to get involved as a third party to try and help parties engaged in disputes to resolve their conflicts. You therefore need to understand the principles of effective mediation and how your role is different to that of other mediators.

Defining mediation

Mediation is a structured process in which an impartial third party facilitates the resolution of a conflict between two negotiating parties. For mediation to be successful, the person selected to mediate a dispute must be acceptable to both of the parties. They must be entirely happy that the mediator is unbiased and will assess the circumstances of the dispute objectively.

If you are asked to mediate a dispute, you need to be certain that you will be able to remain impartial and not let yourself get swept up in the emotional side of what is taking place. Your role will require you to look at the situation from the perspective of each of the disputing parties to find areas of common ground between them, and use this information to make recommendations that would be acceptable to both parties.

ENCOURAGE SELF-DETERMINATION
Ensure that the disputing parties recognize their differences and know that their participation in the mediation process is voluntary and they are free to leave at any time.

GIVE OWNERSHIP
Let the disputing parties know that they must take responsibility for the conflict and for its resolution, and are expected to identify the issues and engage creatively in solving the conflict.

REMAIN NEUTRAL
Ensure that you remain neutral and help to facilitate the mediation process, rather than actively trying to influence the outcomes of the conflict.

Principles of effective mediation

KEEP THE GOAL IN MIND
Always remember that the aim of mediation through integrative negotiation is not to achieve absolute justice, but to develop options and find the most workable and satisfactory option.

ADVOCATE CONFIDENTIALITY
Make it clear to all parties that the mediation process is confidential. Disputing parties are only likely to share important information if they believe that the mediator is neutral and trustworthy.

USE AN INTEGRATIVE APPROACH
Try to understand the interests of each of the disputing parties, and help them reach an integrative (win–win) resolution that they would both find acceptable.

Remaining impartial

The manager's role as a mediator is similar to that of other neutral third-party mediators. He or she is working to the same goal as other mediators: to help the disputing parties resolve their disputes. However, as the types of conflict a manager has to deal with often affect organizational goals and performance, he or she may sometimes find it difficult to remain neutral to its consequences. In order to protect the organization's interests, the manager may sometimes have to exercise more control over how the conflict is mediated and also over how the dispute will be resolved. In addition, managers will often have a shared history and possibly a future relationship with the disputing parties. Given these challenges, a manager must do his or her utmost to mediate the dispute in an unbiased manner.

Understanding the process

The mediation process is a step-by-step, structured process. However, unlike the rigid legal process used for mediation, the process used by managers is flexible. It involves five main steps:
• **Initial contact** Start by meeting with each party to identify the issues and provide general information about the mediation process and principles.
• **Assessment and preparation** Next, you need to introduce your role as the mediator, and talk to each disputing party to obtain information about the nature of the dispute. You should also make an assessment of your ability to mediate this dispute, by deciding whether the disputing parties are ready for mediation. You also need to get the parties to commit to engaging in constructive mediation, by asking them to sign a contract. Finally, make a list of the issues in dispute for later discussion.

• **Joint opening session** Once you are fully prepared, you then need to establish a psychologically safe environment in which the mediation can take place. Clarify the rules of engagement, such as mutual respect, taking notes and meeting privately with each disputing party. Educate the parties on the differences between each of their positions and interests and begin to work on the issues.

• **Joint sessions** Facilitate a productive joint problem-solving situation by continuing to move the disputing parties from positions to interests. Prioritize and narrow down the issues, identify areas of agreement and areas of disagreement, and encourage the disputing parties to make realistic proposals. This may take one or a number of sessions.

• **Agreement** Write down aspects of the agreement as the disputing parties begin to agree on more issues. Ensure that the final agreement is very precise, is owned by the disputants, and is forward-looking.

MEDIATING AS A MANAGER

FAST TRACK	OFF TRACK
Ensuring that the disputing parties reach an integrative agreement that is satisfactory to all	Failing to take the time to fully listen to and understand the interests of the disputing parties
Trying to resolve the conflict as quickly and efficiently as possible	Allowing the conflict to disrupt the organization's day-to-day business
Ensuring that the mediation process is fair to both parties	Introducing your own biases
Allowing disputing parties to express their feelings	Disregarding the emotions of the disputing parties

Learning from the masters

Irrespective of the field in which they practice their trade, be it business, law, diplomacy, labor, or sports, master negotiators possess a unique set of combined characteristics that clearly differentiate them from common negotiators, and define their success. Every negotiator can benefit by understanding the skills and attitudes of a master negotiator.

Becoming a winning negotiator

Master negotiators have superior negotiating capabilities in three major areas: the ability to understand and analyze issues (cognitive skills); the ability to manage emotions, especially negative ones (emotional skills); and the ability to connect with others by developing relationships and trust (social skills). These are the areas that you need to work on if you are to hone your negotiating skills and work toward becoming a master negotiator.

Defining key attributes

The following characteristics are common to all master negotiators:

• **Using masterful due diligence** Master negotiators understand the dangers of being poorly prepared, and invest ample resources in planning and gathering information.

• **Thinking strategically** Negotiations are rarely a one-on-one business, so master negotiators spend time analyzing the interests of the "players" who are not at the table, how the power balance lies, and what opportunities exist to increase their own power.

• **Being firm and flexible** Master negotiators are firm and clear about the issues they must have, and flexible on the issues they would like to have.

• **Seeing the other side** Master negotiators know that they can only present a good offer or trade-off if they know what their counterpart's interests are. They are able to easily shift from seeing things from their point of view to seeing things from that of the other party.

• **Investing in relationships** Master negotiators use all possible opportunities to nurture trust and develop relationships, and make sure that those connections remain intact over time.

• **Managing emotions** Master negotiators make an active choice to always monitor and control their emotions constructively.

• **Appreciating uniqueness** Master negotiators approach every situation afresh and are always ready to modify their practices and adapt to the specific conditions of the current negotiation.

 IN FOCUS... BAD DEALS

Master negotiators know that negotiations are not about making the deal and signing the contract, but rather about diligently pursuing their interests. No deal is better than a bad deal, so they condition themselves mentally to walk away from the table if and when their interests are not met. Inexperienced negotiators tend to be biased toward securing a deal and often tend to stay at the table and get a poor deal. There are two reasons for this: first, negotiators do not want to let go of the sunk costs (expenses) involved in attempting to make the deal. Second, they do not want to face the fact that it simply is not possible to make the deal and thus feel that they have failed to produce results. Master negotiators, in contrast, are willing to let go of the sunk costs and do not feel that they have failed in the negotiation task if the deal does not go through.

Index

Acknowledgments

Author's acknowledgments

Our thanks go to the business associates at the Center for Negotiation (USA) and the International Perspectives (Singapore), to the academic colleagues at Singapore Management University, to our editor Amrit Kaur, and to our research assistant Deborah NG Sui Ling. We appreciate your support. Thanks to the many managers and executives in USA, UK, China, India, Singapore, Thailand, Malaysia, Indonesia, and the Philippines. Your active participation in our negotiation training and coaching workshops put our expertise to the ultimate test of relevancy and precision. Thanks to our students at Johns Hopkins University, Singapore Management University, and Nanyang Technological University, Singapore. Your inquisitive nature helped us crystallize our thinking. Thanks to Marek Walisiewicz, Peter Jones, Kati Dye, and many other talented designers and editors. Your commitment to publish this book gave light to our negotiation and coaching ideas. This collective endeavor will promote the best practice of negotiation.

Publisher's acknowledgments

The publisher would like to thank Hilary Bird for indexing, Judy Barratt for proofreading, and Chuck Wills for coordinating Americanization.

Picture credits

The publisher would like to thank the following for their kind permission to reproduce their photographs:

1 Getty Images: Tipp Howell; 2–3 iStockphoto.com: Marc Brown; 4–5 Getty: Neil Emmerson; 8–9 (background) Alamy: Ken Welsh; 8–9 iStockphoto.com: Clint Scholz; 12 Getty: artpartner-images; 14–15 iStockphoto.com: Aliaksandr Stsiazhyn; 17 iStockphoto.com: Floortje; 20–21 iStockphoto.com: Joshua Blake; 26 iStockphoto.com: Luca di Filippo; 29 iStockphoto.com: Andrew Lilley; 30–31 Alamy Images: Food drink and diet/Mark Sykes; 34 iStockphoto.com: Chris Scredon; 37 iStockphoto.com: 7nuit; 38–39 iStockphoto.com: Lisa Thornberg; 40 iStockphoto.com: Olena Druzhynina; 46–47 Getty Images: Betsie Van der Meer; 53 Corbis: Patti Sapone/Star Ledger; 55 iStockphoto.com: Gary Woodard; 56–57 iStockphoto.com: Perry Kroll; 58–59 iStockphoto.com: blackred; 60 iStockphoto.com: Lise Gagne; 64–65 Getty Images: Ryan McVay; 68 iStockphoto.com: blackred.

Every effort has been made to trace the copyright holders. The publisher apologizes for any unintentional omission and would be pleased, in such cases, to place an acknowledgment in future editions of this book.

About the authors

Dr. Michael Benoliel is Director of the Center for Negotiation (www.centerfornegotiation.com). He has conducted negotiation training in the USA, UK, Singapore, Malaysia, India, Indonesia, Vietnam, Thailand, and the Philippines, and provided negotiation training to companies such as BP, Applied Micro Devices, Prudential, PTT Chemicals, and Mekong Capital. He has taught at Johns Hopkins and Maryland universities, and is currently Associate Professor of Organizational Behavior Practice at Singapore Management University.

Dr. Wei Hua is the founder of the management consulting firm "International Perspectives" (www.international-perspectives.com), and has extensive international experience in research, consulting, training, and teaching in mainland China, Japan, the USA, and Singapore.

Dedication

To my family, Sharon and Talia.
Michael Benoliel

To my dad.
Wei Hua